PUFFIN BOOKS

The Utterly Nutty History of Footy

Martin Chatterton was born in Liverpool in 1961. He has been an illustrator/designer since 1983 and has illustrated over sixty children's books. He is presently a partner in a design company called The Point, in Preston and London. He lives in Southport and is married with two children.

To my wife, Ann,
and to the Gentlemen Players of Birkdale Rovers FC.

PUFFIN BOOKS

Published by the Penguin Group
Penguin Books Ltd, 27 Wrights Lane, London W8 5TZ, England
Penguin Books USA Inc., 375 Hudson Street, New York, New York 10014, USA
Penguin Books Australia Ltd, Ringwood, Victoria, Australia
Penguin Books Canada Ltd, 10 Alcorn Avenue, Toronto, Ontario, Canada M4V 3B2
Penguin Books (NZ) Ltd, 182–190 Wairau Road, Auckland 10, New Zealand

Penguin Books Ltd, Registered Offices: Harmondsworth, Middlesex, England

First published 1997
3 5 7 9 10 8 6 4 2

Made and printed in England by Clays Ltd, St Ives plc

British Library Cataloguing in Publication Data
A CIP catalogue record for this book is available from the British Library

ISBN 0–140–38465–0

The UTTERLY NUTTY History of FOOTY

Written and illustrated by

Martin Chatterton

PUFFIN BOOKS

IN WHAT PROMISES TO BE AN ACTION-PACKED GAME TONIGHT...

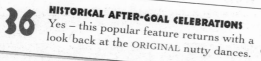

AND OF COURSE, WE'LL ALSO BE BRINGING YOU...

Famous Footballing Fellers, Hysterical Historical Nutty Footy
Facts, **What if Shakespeare...,** Ancient Mysteries Revealed,
Did They Really Say That?, Olde Worlde Footie, **and loads more!**

*Sorry, that should read **Dawkins'** theory,
as in Neil Dawkins of Preston

With just a few minutes to kick off let's take a look at the two line ups. There are few surprises on the team sheet; here's how Good will line up:

God

God   God   God   God

God   God   God

God   God   God

subs: Kenny Dalglish, Alan Shearer, Glenn Hoddle

GOOD

Andy, what do you make of that?

Well, Gary, as you can see, manager Cliff Richard has gone for an attacking 4-3-3 formation and we should expect to see plenty of high balls into the box coming in from Good, as I'm sure Cliff knows Evil has always had difficulty dealing with crosses, a common fault amongst these teams from the Burning Fires of Hell.

I think we'll also see those subs in action if things aren't going well for Good; there was plenty of pre-match controversy about leaving those three on the sidelines and giving their places to The Supreme Being. Let's hope Cliff's picked the right mix; it could be an early bath for the entire universe if they lose this little tussle!

Thanks, Andy. Now here's a quick look at the line up chosen by Darth Vader the Evil manager, recently talked about in connection with the Manchester City job...

Vlad the Impaler

B. Elzebub   Satan   The Lord of Evil   El Diablo

Lou Cifer   Frankenstein   Count Dracul

The Prince of Darkness

EVIL

Wee Darth's gone for a bit of solidity here, Gary. I can see Frankenstein, Dracul and Vlad getting a bit confused today. All three of them think they're God already, so there could be one or two ugly incidents before this match is over!

Thanks, Andy. So stay tuned for action, after the adverts!

ADVERTS FROM FOOTBALL HISTORY

•• 1912 ••

Chums, leave disgusting scenes like this to Johnny Foreigner and avoid unmanly displays of sporting cowardice with The Patented **Jenkins and Windsor Upper Lip Stiffener!**

Made from completely British cast pig iron, the *Lip Stiffener simply bolts on to your head*, preventing your lip from slipping in the event of a rough challenge from a foreign player or harsh treatment from members of the lower classes during a game. (Also available with *'Anti-Pucker Flange'*.)

THE LITTLE KNOWN HISTORY OF DOGS IN FOOTBALL

The Brentford goalie, Chic Brodie, had to give up football completely after a mutt collided with him during a 1970 fixture against Colchester …

In 1985 a dog scored with a diving header in a game between Newcastle Town and Knave of Clubs, two amateur Staffordshire sides. The goal, scored for the Knaves, was allowed and the dog signed on a three-year contract for Man Utd. (Actually, I made that last bit up.)

After being sent off while playing for his club, Corinthians, Brazilian star Edmundo took a video of the game with him to a league hearing to prove his innocence. The video proved nothing, however, as, instead of the footy match, it contained an episode of 'Scooby Doo'!

If it hadn't been for those darned kids I'd have gotten away with it!

Bryn, a police dog, was responsible for saving Torquay from relegation out of the Football League in 1987. In the last game of the season, with a point needed to survive, Torquay were losing 2-1 with seconds remaining. Bryn rushed on and bit the Crewe centre forward. In the time added on to see to the injured player, Torquay scored and stayed up on goal difference ...

In 1966 after the World Cup was pinched, Pickles, a black-and-white mongrel, found the trophy in London.

Harry Cripps, who played for Millwall in the 1960s, was nicknamed 'The Dog'. The Dog, not renowned for his skills, did manage to hold one footballing record: he broke more players' legs than anyone else in League history!

NUTTY FOOTY MUSEUM

Here at **Nutty Footy** one of the greatest collections of footballing history has been gathered together in the **Nutty Footy Museum of Dead Good Stuff.** Painstakingly collected over many years by a dedicated team of hand-picked footballing archaeologists, the Museum is housed in a specially built, temperature-controlled, air-cooled shed at the bottom of the garden.

The Original Halftime Tea Bag

First used in a match between Old Phlegmatics and Bolton Strollers in 1872 and only retired after being ceremonially dunked during the halftime interval in the 1975 FA Cup Final.

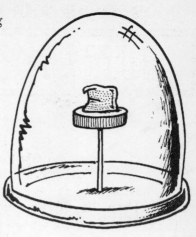

It has been calculated that from this single tea bag, more than six million cuppas have been produced. Famous players who supped on cups from this bag include Nat Lofthouse, Tom Finney, George Best, Bobby Charlton and Danny Blanchflower.

The Killer Ball of Fulham

Before the invention of weather-proof coatings for match balls, case balls like this one were responsible for more deaths than the car. The reason was that, when playing in wet conditions, the old-style ball sucked up water like a sponge, becoming extremely heavy (in one case a ball weighed in at half a ton, about the weight of a small cow).

Add to this the fact that the ball was laced up using tough cord, forming a sort of knuckleduster, it was hardly surprising that games frequently ended in tragedy. This ball was used in a game between Fulham and Chesterfield in 1928, during which 18 of the players, both linesmen and 4 members of the public were killed. The ball escaped and caused panic in Fulham High Road before being subdued by members of the Tooting Fire Brigade.

Peter Beardsley's Teeth

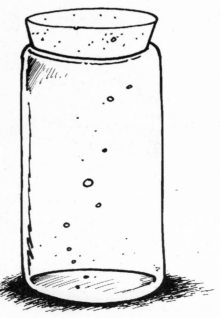

The dazzling Geordie midfielder wasn't always the gummy little tyke you see in post-match interviews. Back in 1985, Peter was involved in a collision with then team-mate Paul Gascoigne. During this collision Beardo's teeth flew out, embedding themselves in a cheese sandwich being eaten by a Mr Gordon Stevens of Gateshead. Mr Stevens happily kept the teeth, and sandwich, on his mantelpiece until kindly donating it for our collection.

Kenny Dalglish's Sense of Humour

Lovable soccer boss, Kenny Dalglish, used to work the cabaret circuit as a stand-up comic before he tragically misplaced his sense of humour at an away fixture in Prague. It showed up many years later after the collapse of the Eastern Bloc countries.

No 1

SOCRATES

Bearded Brazilian doctor and midfield genius, whose main contribution to world thought was to make us wonder how someone so obviously in need of a doctor could deliver such telling balls to Zico. Sometimes confused with Greek bloke from the 5th century BC.

Lone Star, a side from Liberia playing in the Africa Cup, were given an unusual reason to give 100% effort in their next game. If they did not play at their absolute best, said the coach, they would be shot! The result? A goalless draw. Can you imagine what the last few minutes' play must have been like?

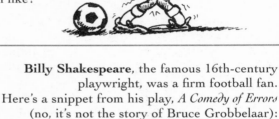

Billy Shakespeare, the famous 16th-century playwright, was a firm football fan. Here's a snippet from his play, *A Comedy of Errors* (no, it's not the story of Bruce Grobbelaar):

'Am I so round with you as you with me,
That like a football you spurn me thus?
You spurn me hence, and he will spurn me hither;
If I last in this service you must case me in leather.'

With players making a bundle of cash from sponsoring football boots, spare a thought for **Abdul Salim**, an Egyptian import who played for Celtic during the 1930s. He insisted on playing without boots and with only bandages wrapped round his feet!

Oi, Rev! In the 19th century the **Reverend Samuel Ashe** thought that Sunday football should be banned. To achieve this he took the unusual step of hiding in bushes during local games, leaping out when the ball came close, then sticking a pin into it!

On the other hand, some clergymen take their love of the beautiful game a little too far. **Canon William de Spalding**, playing in an early (14th-century) game, was involved in an off the ball incident during which he stabbed an opponent to death!

Christmas Day, 1914, German and British soldiers on opposing sides in the First World War call a halt to the fighting so that they can play a game of football. The next day the fighting carries on...

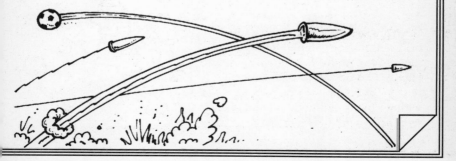

WHAT IF SHAKESPEARE...

Once more
into the box, dear boys,
once more;
Or chuck the ball up to the edge of
the 'D'. At halftime there's nothing so
becomes a lad
As some biccies and a cup of tea.
But when the ref's whistle blows in our ears
Then imitate the action of The Shearer;
Stiffen the shinpads, dubbin up your boots,
Disguise fair nature with hard-favour'd rage
(Except for you, Darren, you just try it the other way)
And give the ball some right welly
Let it fly into the back of the onion bag
Dead fast like. Let this lot overwhelm you
And you can all stay in after school tomorrow.
Now set the teeth and stretch the nostrils wide
Robbie Fowler style, and bend up every spirit
To his full height! On, on, you mighty sprogs!
I see you stand like greyhounds in the slips,
Straining upon the start. The game's afoot:
Follow your spirit; and, upon this charge,
Cry 'Goal for Year 3!
East Cheam and St George's
Primary Under 11s!'

the X fools! >

The Strange Case of Emerson's Hair

October 1996. England. Doctors up and down the country start to notice a rise in the number of people suddenly going completely rigid. The cases all have two things in common: firstly, the stiffness strikes without warning and, secondly, all the incidents happen at football matches involving Middlesbrough FC. The initial mystery is why these events only happen at certain games ...

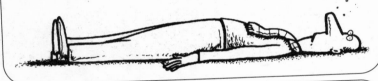

Agent Mouldy studied the match statistics and fed them through the FBI supercomputer at head-quarters in Langley, Virginia. Something was troubling him. He ran his fingers through his thick Hollywood hair.

Agent Scally, meanwhile, ran straight to a dark, spooky, secret research station and began to open creaking, metal doors. It had nothing to do with the case, but Scally knew that until one of them had been into a really scary building, no File could ever be solved!

Back at Langley, the supercomputer had crunched some numbers and found one interesting fact: all the incidents had happened when the Brazilian star Emerson was playing! Mouldy thought hard; what was the connection between Emerson and the stiff people? Why didn't the Brazilian have a first name? And why did Bryan Robson sell Nick Barmby to Everton? Mouldy thought he knew the answer to the first two questions and picked up his cute little mobile phone.

Scally? Mouldy here. Get down to the British Museum and meet me in the Ancient Greek section, oh, and Scally?

Yes?

Wear your sunglasses.

The Strange Case of Emerson's Hair << CLASSIFIED >> 2

At the museum Mouldy stood in front of a Greek carving, holding a photograph of Emerson. Scally looked over his shoulder at the carving. It showed a hideous head, with hissing snakes instead of hair.

Look, Scally. This is an ancient carving showing the Medusa, a mythical Greek monster – she turned people who gazed upon her to stone! And look, here's Emerson. Look at the resemblance! Emerson has become a modern-day Medusa! Clear evidence of interzonal-extrachronological time shifting!

I'm sorry, Mouldy, I've been doing a bit more digging and I think there's a reasonable explanation for the Emerson case.

ANCIENT MYSTERIES REVEALED...

Stonehenge

For centuries the arguments have raged amongst scientists and historians about the mysterious stone circle in Wiltshire. Was it the secret spiritual home of ancient mystics?

A prehistoric interplanetary reception station?

OR, THE FIRST ALL-SEATER FOOTY STADIUM IN WILTSHIRE?

Yes, now it can be revealed: the ring of stones, long thought to contain some deep and meaningful mystery, was in fact a Stone Age Wembley! With full seating for as many as 26 footy fans at a time, Stonehenge was the venue for every FA Cup Final for 10,052 years. It stopped being used after the bad-tempered final between Glastonbury Wanderers and Ton Petrie Druids led to a pitch invasion.

EXPLORERS,

THE TRUTH BEHIND THE LEGENDS

Many people have thrilled to the exploits of the brave explorers who boldly go where no man has gone before (including away games at Millwall) and do what men have to do and all that heroic bit. In reality, there were very good reasons why these famous explorers went where they went. Here's the truth ...

1. CHRISTOPHER COLUMBUS

The legend:

Italian explorer who, defying popular and scientific opinion that the world was flat, sailed west, discovering the American continent and claiming it for the Spaniards, who had backed him.

A NUTTY FOOTY SPECIAL

The truth:

Columbus had been signed from Fiorentina by Spanish giants, Barcelona. However, an argument with the Barca manager led to Columbus signing a massive contract to play for the newly formed American Soccer League club, Milwaukee Maulers.

The legend:

Whilst on Scott's brave but doomed attempt to reach the South Pole, Captain Oates left the shelter of his tent to face certain death in the sub-zero temperatures, in order that his comrades might survive. His last words were: 'I might be some time!'

The truth:

'Captain' Oates was in fact captain of QPR, the last remaining British team playing in Europe that season. After being knocked out by a late goal, the team got lost returning from a second round, second leg away tie to Dukla Prague. With no hotel in sight they established base camp using the goalie's jersey as a makeshift tent.

Oates *really* left the team tent to see if he could call a minicab. He couldn't find one and bought a dodgy kebab from Stig's Kebab Hut, contracted food poisoning and never made it back.

The legend:

Heroic British sailor who charted the New Zealand coastline, landed in Australia at Botany Bay and was killed by islanders after landing in Hawaii.

The truth:

Jimmy Cook was actually not a seafaring type of captain at all. He was, in fact, captain of Portsmouth FC. Before a crucial Inter-Toto Cup game in Genoa, Jimmy was the victim of a practical joke: his team-mates tied him up and put him on board a ship which was due to sail that day. The crew, seeing his captain's armband, assumed he was the Captain Cook they had been waiting for and set sail. The real Captain Cook turned up half an hour later and was mistaken for the missing Portsmouth centre half. He played against Genoa, scoring a glancing header in a 2-2 draw.

OUCH!

UTTERLY NUTTY INJURIES

All footballers know that once in a while they will pick up a thigh strain, pull a muscle or tweak a hamstring. These injuries are part and parcel of the game. However, a quick trawl through the archives reveals a horrifying catalogue of completely nutty injuries that, despite the pain they cause the unlucky player, still give us a dead good laff!

Gordon Petric of Glasgow Rangers needed treatment after being bitten on the elbow by his own goalie, Andy Goram!

Hadjuk Split star, Milan Rapaic, was sidelined when he jabbed a boarding pass in his eye at an airport!

Nick Holmes, the Southampton midfielder, had to leave the field when he tripped over an ants' nest!

Amateur player Royston Marley missed a vital game after a group of chickens pecked his knees!

Peter Whitehurst, playing for Grantham Town, had his ear stapled to his head by his ear-ring in a game against Norwich City!

Tranmere's Shaun Teale suffered a badly gashed arm after cleaning out a fish tank!

Goalie Dave Beasant was out after DROPPING a jar of salad cream on his toe!

Famous Arsenal striker Charlie George sliced off one of his toes with a lawnmower!

Alan Mullery, the former midfielder for Tottenham and England, put his back out doing that most dangerous of daily tasks: brushing his teeth!

Finally, spare a thought for the Indonesian player Mistar who, during a training session, was KILLED by a rampaging gang of pigs that invaded the pitch!

FAMOUS FOOTBALLING FELLERS

No 2

ALBERT CAMUS

Dead hip (and, er, actually dead) cult French existentialist* novelist, most famous for writing *The Stranger* and for a last-minute fingertip save while playing as France's only existentialist goalie. 'All that I know surely about morality and the obligations of man, I owe most surely to football.'

* existentialism: means that after you die, there is nothing except a match between Arsenal and Leeds in which the score stays at 0-0. For infinity.

HISTORICAL AFTER-GOAL CELEBRATIONS

In previous Nutty Footy books (WHADDYA MEAN, you haven't read them?) we have shown some of the best and nuttiest ways of celebrating scoring a goal. Who can forget modern classics like 'The Pooch', ' The Crooner' or 'The Fighter Pilot'?

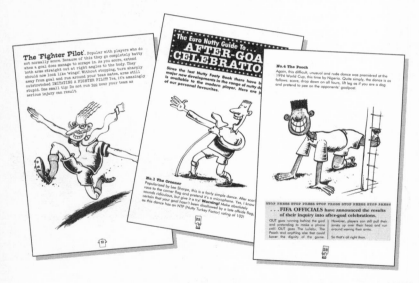

The 'Fighter Pilot'. Popular with players who do not normally score. Because of this they go completely batty when a goal does manage to scrape in. As you score, extend both arms straight out at right angles to the body. They should now look like 'wings'. Without stopping, turn sharply away from goal and run around your team mates, arms still outstretched IMITATING A FIGHTER PILOT. Yes, it's amazingly stupid. One small tip: Do not run too near your team as serious injury can result.

The Euro Nutty Guide To AFTER-GOAL CELEBRATIO

Since the last Nutty Footy Book there have b major new developments in the range of nutty d is available to the modern player. Here are j of our personal favourites.

No.1 The Crooner
Popularized by Lee Sharpe, this is a fairly simple dance. After scor race to the corner flag and pretend it's a microphone. Yes, I know sounds ridiculous, but give it a try! **Warning!** Make absolutely certain that your goal hasn't been disallowed by a late offside flag, as this dance has an NTF (Nutty Turkey Factor) rating of 10!

25

No.4 The Pooch
Again, this difficult, unusual and rude dance was premiered at the 1994 World Cup, this time by Nigeria. Quite simply, the dance is as follows: score, drop down on all fours, lift leg as if you are a dog and pretend to pee on the opponents' goalpost.

STOP PRESS STOP PRESS STOP PRESS STOP PRESS STOP PRESS
... FIFA OFFICIALS have announced the results of their inquiry into after-goal celebrations.

OUT goes running behind the goal and pretending to make a phone call! OUT goes The Lullaby. The Pooch and anything else that could lower the dignity of the game.

However, players can still pull their jersey up over their head and run around waving their arms.

So that's all right then.

26

Extracts from The Nutty Footy Book ©1994, The Euro Nutty Footy Book ©1996

But things weren't always like this. The Nutty Footy research team has been trawling through the history books to find out how goals were celebrated in times gone by ...

N°1
The Gentleman's Apology

When the game of football as we know it began during the reign of Queen Victoria, it was played mainly by amateurs. These upper-class gentlemen considered any form of emotional display after scoring to be rather vulgar, jolly bad form and the act of a complete bounder. So, even after sprinting the length of the park, turning the defence inside out and thrashing a volley into the top corner in front of 197,000 fans to score the winning goal in the Cup Final, a true gentleman player would simply turn away from goal, replace his monocle, adjust his cravat, nod apologetically to the opposing captain and stroll back to the centre circle.

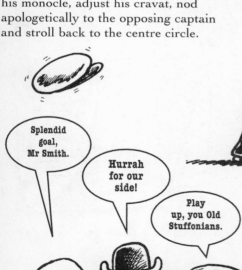

> Splendid goal, Mr Smith.

> Hurrah for our side!

> Play up, you Old Stuffonians.

Mind you, the crowd weren't much better. Polite applause, mild comments and hat tossing were the only acceptable levels of behaviour (see diagram).

Nº2
The Handshake

By the 1930s things had moved on … but not much. Players were no longer gentlemen amateurs. They were honest hardworking gritty blokey-type blokes, who got the bus to the ground on match days, carried their own boots and trained on a diet of lard pies and stout. On the field there was only one way of celebrating a goal: a firm, manly handshake for your team-mates, followed by a brisk jog back up the pitch.

Nº3
The Loony Rabbit

1966. England's finest hour. In dramatic fashion the boys in red lift the most coveted prize in world football by beating Germany 4 goals to 2. It was during this game that Nobby Stiles (yes, really, someone called 'Nobby' did play for England back then) perfected this celebration. You roll your socks right down, let your shirt hang loose, remove your three front teeth (you can skip this part if you are a bit of a wuss) and just leap up and down in a kind of bunny hop, waving your hands in the air.

Nº4
The Snogger

After the swinging Sixties and the brazen exhibitionism of Nobby Stiles, the floodgates opened and players could dance about after scoring as much as they liked. However, there were a few players who went a little too far and, er, well, they, er … well basically they started snogging after scoring. All right, there, I've said it. Usually it was pop-star sort of players like Alan Hudson and Rodney Marsh, who played for soft glamour clubs like Chelsea or QPR, who planted a smooch on the face of the scorer. There were a couple of nasty incidents at Liverpool and Leeds in the 1970s when players tried to kiss Tommy 'Iron Man' Smith and Norman 'Bites Yer Legs' Hunter on the rare occasions these two plug-uglies found the net.

No 3

MAO TSE-TUNG

Controversial chairman of Beijing FC from 1948 to 1976. Believed to be responsible for the introduction of the red card into football and for starting the chant heard at Liverpool and Man Utd: 'Red Army! Red Army! Red Army! Red Army!...'

The fastest attacks in footy history must have been those mounted during the 1930s when a craze for **motorcycle football** swept the nation! Teams of six played at speeds of more than 60 miles an hour watched by large crowds…

More loony behaviour: **Joey Goodchild** was a popular halftime performer at Watford FC in the 1920s, where he regularly entertained the punters with a spot of tap dancing… on the roof of the main stand! This was all going spiffingly for Joey until he managed to fall off the roof. Luckily his fall was cushioned by a couple in the crowd (not so lucky for them, I suppose).

Phew! That was lucky!

When the ancient **Aztecs** played footy, goals were very scarce. Just as well really, because any player who scored was allowed to keep the clothes and possessions of any of the spectators!

②

Hristo Stoichkov, the miserable but talented Bulgarian genius, comes from a town called Ysno Pole where the townspeople want the name changed to Stoichkovo in his honour.

Don Bell of Bradford Park Avenue was the only footballing professional to win the Victoria Cross, Britain's highest medal for bravery, during World War I.

When **Arbroath** stuffed Bon Accord 36-0 in 1885, the Arbroath keeper never touched the ball. In fact he watched the game from the shelter of an umbrella!

Brazilian club **Londrina** pays win bonuses to its players by giving them... cows.

Nutty names revisited: '**Mysterious Dwarfs FC**' used to play in Ghana's first division.

To 4-3-3 or not to 4-3-3,
that is the question.
Whether 'tis nobler in the mind to suffer
the slings and arrows of some absolutely
outrageous refereeing,
Or, to play a big feller against a sea of red jerseys
And by opposing end them? – Today? – Too sloppy.
No more: and, by sloppy, I say we end
The heartache and the thousand natural shocks
That fans are heir to – 'tis summat the lads have been
Really working on in training. To draw, to win:-
To win! perchance to dream: ay there's the rub.
For in that final run in to the championship
what draws may come,
When we have shuffled off this mortal coil,
Sorta makes you think a bit,
eh Brian?

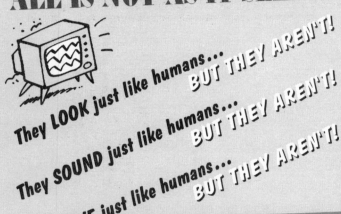

A high-level Nutty Alien Investigation Unit has been operating a deep-cover covert surveillance operation since a trace signal from a parallel universe was intercepted and translated (oh all right, we just slumped in front of the gogglebox and watched the footy).

The footy itself showed no sign of alien activity (except perhaps the sight of David James in an England shirt).

But we did notice some rather disturbing things happening during the halftime discussions. To put it bluntly, **we believe that some of our footballers are being bodysnatched and replaced by invaders from Mars!**

Here's the evidence:

CASE #01BOD.LIN
When Gary Lineker first became a panellist he was the typical boy next door.

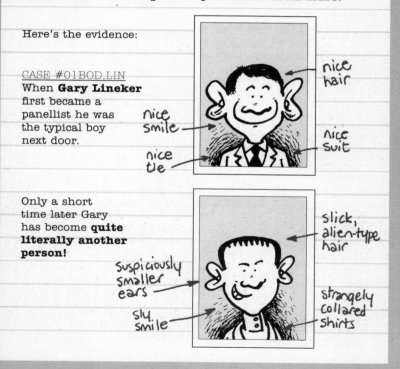

Only a short time later Gary has become **quite literally another person!**

CASE #02BOD.VEN

Take Sky Sport's **Barry Venison** (please, somebody TAKE BARRY VENISON!). The ex-Liverpool, Newcastle and Southampton midfielder used to be famous for his outrageous appearance. Here's what he looked like in early broadcasts:

astonishingly vile haircut

amazingly horrible jacket... shirts... trousers...

Last week I switched on and Barry Venison, King of the Disco, had become **Professor B. Venison!**

blimey!

CASE #03BOD.HAN

Alan Hansen used to be a dour, straight-talking ex-Liverpool defender with a strong resemblance to Count Dracula.

Now he's a jovial, chubby and talkative practical joker and the **life and soul of the party!***

*actually we made that last bit up.

48

ANCIENT MYSTERIES REVEALED...

The Pyramids

Rising mysteriously from the Nile delta landscape, the great pyramids of Egypt contained undreamt-of treasures: gold, emeralds, rubies, beautiful carvings and the tombs of the Great Kings – Mykerinus, Khephren and, the greatest of all, Kheops... *or so we thought!*

In fact the great pyramids were the dressing rooms for *Athletico Cairo FC*, a fabulously wealthy team of the time. The body of Kheops is that of Cairo's record signing, Al-Anshe-ra, and the contents of the pyramid are the signing-on fee.

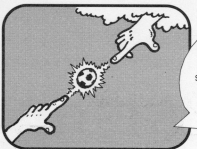

In the beginning there was the ball. Or at least, a roundish kind of stone. Rival prehistoric social groups, instead of leathering one another over hunting arguments, began to leather one another over footy games. To have a game of footy there is one essential ingredient: *a ball*.

Early experimental footballs proved useless.

There is some evidence that *football hooliganism* began around this time; just take a look at this prehistoric cave painting.

After the introduction of the round stone by the FA's Graham Kelly (that's right, the miserable one who picks the Cup draw), the prehistoric game progressed rapidly. A league sprang up of three teams. As the population of the planet was only 33, this meant that everybody had to play.

The league's most respected referee was a Mr T. Rex who never booked or sent off a single player, unless you count eating them.

It wasn't until around about 2500 BC that the Chinese started using footballs made from animal skins in a game which also saw the introduction of goals: 30 FEET HIGH! You can imagine the problems that the keeper faced. The game, called 'tsu chu', was also used to train the Emperor's army.

This was all very well except that during important battles the Chinese army all went for a shower after 90 minutes!

In America, native Indians began the trend towards groovy kit design during their games of 'pasuckuakohowog', a real mouthful which roughly means 'they gather to play ball with the foot'. The players dressed up in ornaments and body paint in games lasting several days and usually resulting in many injuries.

Further north, Eskimos played footy on the ice, with games called off if the weather was too good!

Pacific islanders played using coconuts for balls. Imagine connecting with a header...

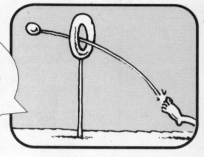

... perhaps news of this spread to Central America, where a rubber ball was first used in a game which involved kicking the ball through a stone ring.

Ye olde worlde telle

ROMA 0
LITTLE PUDDLEBY 2

Meanwhile, over in England, a game involving entire villages was becoming very popular. In fact, there was an early European tie between an English village playing against a team of Romans, beating them and running them out of town! This would be rather like a team such as Torquay, for example, beating AC Milan.

The game continued to grow, with no rules of any kind, except that there were no rules! Injuries were common, and severe.

When football began to interfere with archery training, the first of a procession of royal bans was handed out (see page 60).

By 1863, however, the first rules were drawn up, and the English FA was born.

The game quickly spread around the globe, with about 39 million players worldwide!

One of those players was Kenny Dalglish! I think that proves my theory. Thank you for watching. Goodnight.

ADVERTS FROM FOOTBALL HISTORY

•• 1883 ••

chafing occurs here

x

Doctors,

anxious about the epidemic of injuries caused by today's **woolly footer shorts** ~ *(see diagram)* ~ chafing gentlemen's legs, have arrived at a solution which we are now able to *pass on to the public.*

x

Ease the pain caused by chafing shorts with

FLEMINGS MEDICATED SHORT CHAFING LOTION

Just rub gently into those areas of the anatomy flayed by your footer bags and feel the pain melt away.

ANCIENT MYSTERIES REVEALED...

The Great Wall of China

The only man-made object visible from outer space, the Great Wall stretches for 1490 miles across northern China and was long thought to have been built to keep out hostile invaders from the north...

... the reality is slightly different! When England were drawn in the same World Cup qualifying group as China, the football authorities, anxious to prevent soccer violence, got a bit carried away with the stadium perimeter fence...

FAMOUS FOOTBALLING FELLERS

No 4

I ♥ FOOTY

NIETZSCHE

Friedrich Nietzsche – the German coach who argued for the survival of the fittest and went on to manage Watford and develop the long ball game.

'HOW MUCH *£$?'

Nowadays your club will have to stump up a zillion quid just to get a flabby right-back with a dodgy knee. Top-class talent commands breathtaking fees: £15 million and rising.

However, it wasn't always like this: you used to be able to pick up very decent players for less than the price of a bag of chips and still have change for a can of Coke. Here's the Nutty guide to the rising cost of footy talent…

£££

Alf Common was the first transfer record breaker, moving from Sheffield United to Sunderland for £520 in 1904. A year later he smashed his own record by moving to Middlesbrough for £1000.

By 1922 Syd Puddefoot(!) was transferred from West Ham to Falkirk for a record £5000. Four years later that was doubled when David Jack went from Bolton Wanderers to Arsenal for £10000.

£££

In 1938 one newspaper suggested that the transfer of Bryn Jones to Wolves marked a high point in transfer fees that would never be broken. The fee? £14000!

£££

By 1947 Tommy Lawton had proved that wrong in a £20000 move from Chelsea to Notts County.

It was when clubs from overseas joined the action that records began to rise rapidly.

£££

In the 1950s John Charles moved to Juventus for £65000 and Denis Law became the first £100000 player, going from Manchester City to Torino.

The next big hurdle was the million pound mark, which was passed in 1979 when Trevor Francis left Birmingham for Notts Forest. Many other million pounders followed in the next decade.

£££

By 1992 Kenny Dalglish bought Alan Shearer for a record £3.6 million in what now looks like the bargain of the century!

£££

In Britain the records continued to rise, with Andy Cole (£7 million) and Stan Collymore (£8 million) both becoming big-money flops.

£££

Abroad, records were paid for (amongst others) Ruud Gullit and Diego Maradona. Gianluca Vialli was a notable one, moving to Juventus for £13 million.

In 1996 Alan Shearer once again upped the stakes when Newcastle paid an astonishing £15 million to Blackburn.

At the other end of the scale:

Jack Spelton cost Holt United 30 sheets of corrugated iron!

Blackpool bought William Wright in 1951 for a complete set of orange shirts!

Tony Cascarino, who played in two World Cups and for Marseille, was once swapped for a set of tracksuits!

Uruguayan Daniel Allende moved from Rentistas to Central Espanol in 1979 for 550 beef steaks!

Hughie McLenahan went to Manchester United for a few fridges full of ice cream!

FOOTBALL & ROYALTY

You may think that the connection between football and royalty is limited to shaking hands with the teams on Cup Final day, or with the fact that Prince Charles is a dead ringer for the FA Cup itself (see diagram), but you would be mistaken.

THE FA CUP   PRINCE CHARLES

In fact, attending big games is only a fairly recent event, first happening in 1914, when George V presented the trophy to Burnley.

Before this, most royals tended to be firmly of the opinion that footy was A BAD THING, with the game being banned by King Edward II in 1314:

Forasmuch as there is great noise in the city caused by hustling over large balls, from which many evils may arise, which God forbid, we command and forbid on behalf of the King, on pain of imprisonment, such game to be used in the city in future.

eh?

When football became increasingly popular it had one side effect which annoyed many British monarchs, including Edward III and Henry IV: it began to interfere with archery practice.

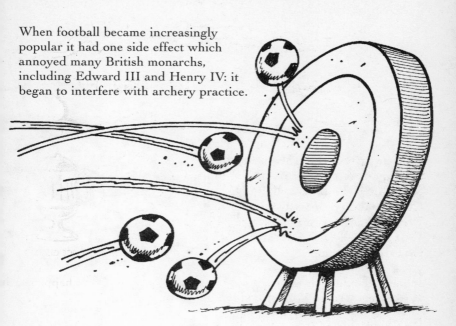

Elizabeth I and James I also banned the game from London and the court, and it wasn't until Charles II watched a top-flight Italian Serie A game in Florence that a royal showed any positive interest in the sport. Of course, nothing has changed since then; Italian football was still dead good but *totally* boring after a while.

Resultos:

Ye Olde Fiorentina	0	Ye Olde Roma	0
Ye Olde Milano	0	Ye Olde Lazio	0
Ye Olde Piacenza	0	Ye Olde Juventus	0
Ye Olde Napoli	0	Ye Olde Torino	0

Other interesting royal stuff:

Note – only **three** of these bits of nonsense are actually true, but which ones? (Answers are on the opposite page.)

The Knights of the Round Table, **King Arthur**'s sturdy noblemen, were in fact an early FA committee. The tradition is continued to this day, with all members of the committee wearing full armour. ①

② **King Cetawayo** and his brother Dabulamanzi of the Zulus played in a side which toured Britain in 1879 and beat Sheffield United 5-4.

Queen Victoria was a Subbuteo nut! She used to hold full tournaments in secret, under her voluminous petticoats! ③

King Henry VIII ④ managed the highly successful women's Cup-winning side of 1541.

You're playing like a bunch of headless chickens!

Prince Charles once played left back for Rotherham, scoring on his home debut in a 3-1 win over Barnsley. (5)

Reading FC's nickname (6) is **The Royals.**

The illustrator would like to apologize for not being able to think of anything funny for this picture.

The 'Real' in 'Real Madrid' actually means **'Royal'** in Spanish. King Juan Carlos (7) is a club member.

Kevin Keegan's haircut during the 1970s was a copy of that made popular by the French **King Louis XIV** when he played for Paris St-Germain. (8)

the X fools!

Watch The Pies!

January 24th 1996. Preston, England. 3.45pm.
As the cheers of the crowd watching Preston's first half against Bury faded, Stu Rowlands, a fitter's mate from Lostock Hall, slipped from his seat in the Tom Finney stand and made his way to the pie stall for his usual halftime meal: two meat and potato pies and a cup of tea. His companion, Tony Roberts, an undertaker's assistant, requested a Cadbury's Wispa.

CLASSIFIED

Stu never returned...

January 26th 1996.
The Preston FBI Office behind the BettaBuy superstore, 9am.

Agent Mouldy took a nervous bite from the meat and potato pie in his hand. A slow smile played across his features.

'What is it Mouldy?' asked Agent Scally.
'It's mouldy,' said Mouldy. 'Exactly what you'd expect from a three-day-old meat and potato pie. But this pie has been held in the Preston FBI food laboratory deep freeze in sterile conditions! It should be perfect! And listen, earlier, when I bit into the pie I could have sworn I heard a tiny scream! I have an idea I know what happened to Stu Rowlands...'

Watch The Pies! << CLASSIFIED >> **2**

I think that these pies are alien spaceships that look like meat and potato pies. They've been planning an invasion of Earth, using football matches as a starting point. The aliens themselves feed on human flesh! Rowlands saw one of them leave the pie spaceship and they killed and ate him to stop him blowing their cover.

Scally looked at Mouldy, her head on a cooky little slant so that the light caught her attractive green, Hollywood eyes. 'Meet me outside Ashworth Hospital, in a couple of hours, I've got a little checking to do,' she said, darting out into the Lancashire drizzle.

Ashworth High Security Hospital, Merseyside, 11am.

Agent Mouldy checked his watch and paced impatiently outside the control gate. Suddenly Scally appeared from inside the hospital with two men in white coats.

'Hi, Scally,' said Mouldy, 'have you come up with anything on this Alien Meat and Potato Pie Case?'

'Sure, Mouldy,' said Agent Scally. 'I've been fishing around in the area and I paid a visit to Rowlands' pal Tony Roberts at work. Remember he's an undertaker's assistant? Well, on a hunch I asked him to open the caskets and there was Stu Rowlands, dead as a doornail. Apparently he owed money to Roberts and they'd argued over it. Roberts stiffed Rowlands. Case closed.'

'Wow!' said Mouldy. 'But there's one thing I don't understand: if the case is closed why are we here at this high security mental institution?'

'Because you're nutty as a fruitcake, sunshine, and I've had you committed. Take him away, boys!'

As Mouldy struggled with the two nurses, Scally sighed and turned towards her car.

MORE NUTTY NAMES!

The history of the glorious game is littered with totally potty team names. We took a look at some of the better foreign efforts in EuroNutty Footy but what about our own wonderfully stupid collection of team names? Let's take a look...

Some of the best-known teams began life as something entirely different.

When **Everton** first began playing, both they and **Liverpool** were part of the same club and were known as **St Domingo's FC**!

Manchester United played under the rather dull name of **Newton Heath** from 1878 to 1902...

... while neighbours **Manchester City** were known as **Ardwick FC**.

Arsenal began life as **Dial Square** before switching to the slightly less nutty **Royal Arsenal**, then to **Woolwich Arsenal**, then to **The Arsenal** before finally making their minds up in 1927, when they became plain old **Arsenal**!

Newcastle United played under the very silly title of **Stanley** until 1892. Still it could have been worse, they could have decided to call themselves *Nigel*, or *Colin*...

From 1883 to 1898 **Coventry City** played under the musical name of **Singer's FC** ... not because they were particularly tuneful but because they were formed by workers from the nearby *Singer's Bicycle Factory*.

And, on an industrial theme, **West Ham United** started life as **Thames Ironworks**.

So much for the top flight. What about those sides lower down the leagues?

Oldham Athletic played as **Pine Villa**...

Gillingham as **Excelsior**...

Bolton Wanderers as **Christ Church Sunday School FC**...

But outside the professional leagues is where you get the real gems.

Real Ale Madrid, A3 Milan, PSV Hangover, JCB Eindhoven, Inter Thevalley, AFC Bacon Sandwich and **Borussia Munchenflapjack** are all *real* amateur British teams!

TIME TRAVELLERS!

If you're making a trip back through time and fancy a bit of a kick about, you can improve your chances with Nutty Footy's...

HISTORICAL HINTS!

No.1 The Garden of Eden

Make sure you pack a long scarf.

No.2 The Stone Age

Always use a regulation FIFA approved leather and polypropolene mix ball, not something that looks like it might be a ball.

No.3 The Roman Empire

Get hold of a big pair of
shinpads when playing
away at the Coliseum.

No.4 The Vikings

Use only the non-horned
type of Viking
helmet.

No.5 Medieval England

Be prepared for local pitch variations.

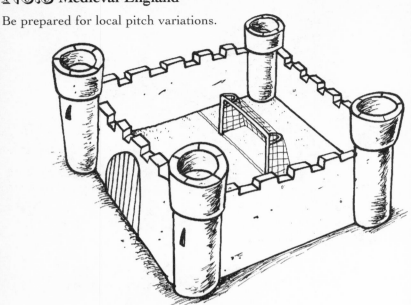

No.6 15th-Century Spain

Try not to get too involved when
the Spanish Inquisition are
refereeing.

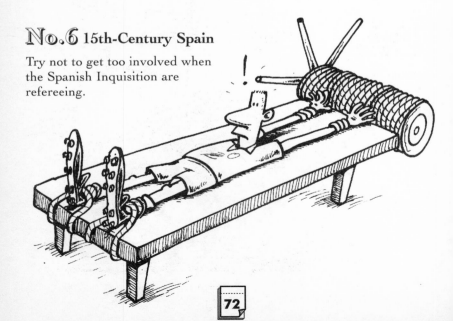

No.7
16th-Century England

Take a decent pair of shorts to avoid a high turkey factor.

No.8
The Wild West

Avoid penalty shoot-outs at all costs.

Shall I compare
thee to a summer's day?
Thou art more lovely and more likely
to bang a couple in:
Rough backs do hack the darling
boots of Alan,
And your contract's up in all too short a date.
Sometime too hot the 'Serie A' shines,
And often comes up with a right attractive offer
That, to be fair, you've so far declined.
But thy eternal strike rate shall not fade,
Nor will you lose possession in and around the box,
Nor shall defenders brag thou wer'st
in their pockets,
When in eternal lines your goal tally grow'st;
So long as men can breathe,
or eyes can see,
They'll all be after you, Alan.
PLEASE sign for me!

We was robbed! In 1991 top Uruguayan rivals Penarol and Nacional were playing in an action-packed derby game. As players jostled for a corner, **Goncalves** of Penarol and **Valdez** of Nacional were involved in a tussle. Nobody at the ground saw a thing but TV cameras spotted Goncalves pull a gold chain from Valdez and hide it in his sock! After the game police picked up the thieving defender!

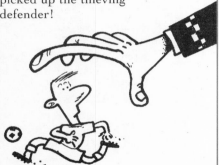

Cumbernauld United, a part-time Scottish outfit, were once lucky enough to have the legendary Kenny Dalglish playing for them. Faced with the selection problems of choosing a position for a player who would become one of the greatest-ever strikers in world football, the Cumbernauld manager had no hesitation. Dalglish was played… in goal!

Whenever **Preston North End** get relegated, their fans bury a coffin representing the death of their dreams. When Preston win promotion they dig it up again.

Sir William Jordan of Chitterne in Wiltshire had a football on his family's coat of arms as long ago as the early 1600s.

NUTTY FOOTY FACTS

3

Eskimos played footy on ice with a ball stuffed with caribou hair and goals 10 MILES apart!

In a 1994 Cup match, **Barbados** had to beat **Grenada** by two clear goals to go through. With five minutes left, Barbados, although 2-1 up, were making little progress and looked like going out. However, if the game was drawn and then won on penalties, the winners were awarded a 2-0 victory. Realizing they had only to score an own goal Barbados started attacking their own net! Grenada found themselves having to defend BOTH goals at the same time!

Team-mates playing for a Bristol amateur team in 1989 were puzzled when **Mike Bennett**, their keeper, made no effort to save an easy shot. The reason? Mike had frozen to the spot and had to be taken off, suffering from hypothermia!

Midland Peking Rendezvous FC (yes, really!) dropped their keeper, 20-year-old Tony Chadwick, after spotting him chomping on a bacon butty during a game against local rivals Thatched Cottage FC (!)! 'I did keep a clean sheet,' moaned Tubby Tony …

THE LONG

Nutty historians have known for some time that the 13th-century Mongol Empire created by the infamous Genghis Khan used a 3-5-2 formation to top the table.

In this Nutty Quiz just put in the first letter of each answer to find out the ancient Mongol battle-cry!

Clues

1. Euro 96 Champions?
2. East Anglian club who aren't Norwich?
3. Wimbledon 'hard man'?
4. Liverpool's 'School of Science' ?
5. In what country would you watch 'Serie A' games?
6. Ex-England, Tottenham and Barcelona manager?

CROSS**WORD**

7. Who are 'The Owls'?
8. Manchester United's ground?
9. The team that Roy of the Rovers plays for?
10. Dodgy film in which Sly Stallone plays as goalie in a team which includes Michael Caine, Pele, Bobby Moore, Ossie Ardiles and John Wark!?
11. England's home ground?
12. 30 minutes played at end of drawn Cup matches?
13. QPR's ground?
14. Italian club who bought Paul Gascoigne?
15. Colour of the card produced for a booking?

DID THEY REALLY SAY THAT?

THE NUTTY FOOTY HISTORY OF INSULTS...

'I am 100% sure our fans won't abuse Cantona. For a start, Manchester United haven't given us any tickets.'

John Barnes,
Liverpool

'Every thousandth person created, God unhinges their heads, scoops out their brains and then issues them to a football club as supporters.'

Mike Bateson,
Torquay chairman

'They are dogs, worms, vermin.'

Joe Kinnear talking about football agents

'The referee today was a muppet.'

Ian Wright,
Arsenal

'Lots of footballers don't have a high IQ to start with, so it would be difficult to gauge the effects of heading the ball too much.'

John Colquhoun,
Hearts

'I never wanted to be a coach because I've a low opinion of players. Footballers are the most obnoxious, ignorant and selfish people.'

Edwin Stein,
Birmingham coach

'He's tiny. I half expected him to go out with a school satchel on his back. If he had I would have trod on his packed lunch.'

Andy Thorn, Wimbledon (about Juninho)

'The man is obviously a few sandwiches short of a picnic.'

Reg Burr, Millwall chairman (about Ian Wright)

'The lasting memory I have of him is that he always had a runny nose.'

Dave Mogg, Bath City keeper talking about his old manager, Roy Hodgson

'Ken Bates paid £1 for Chelsea. He was done.'

Barry Hearn, Orient chairman

'They call him Big Ron because he is a big spender in the transfer market. I just call him Fat Ron.'

Malcolm Allison, Bristol Rovers' then manager

'My heart is with United, but I can't stay for one reason – and that's the manager.'

Andrei Kanchelskis, Fiorentina (talking about Alex Ferguson)

'I wouldn't go so far as to say he's a complete nutcase, but he comes very close to it.'

Terry Yorath (about Neville Southall)

'The best way to watch Wimbledon is on Ceefax.'

Gary Lineker

ANCIENT MYSTERIES REVEALED...

Easter Island

The reason behind the 500 gigantic, mysterious, stone carved heads on the tiny Pacific island has baffled brainy people for, oh, ages. Now Nutty Footy research teams have unravelled the puzzle of the gloomy statues gazing glumly out to sea. They are in fact a monument erected by Dutch supporters after the trouncing they were given by England during the 1996 European Championships! Just compare this photograph of Dirk Van Hire, a Dutch supporter from Rotterdam, and the photograph of an Easter Island head.

FAMOUS FOOTBALLING FELLERS

No 5

LENIN

Key player in the Russian Revolution of 1917 when Dynamo Moscow dramatically switched formation from 4-4-2 to 3-5-2. With Lenin given a free role behind the front two (Stalin and Trotsky), the 'Red Army' scored notable victories against their deadly rivals, Leeds United (the 'White Army').

TOMORROW'S ANTIQUES TODAY!

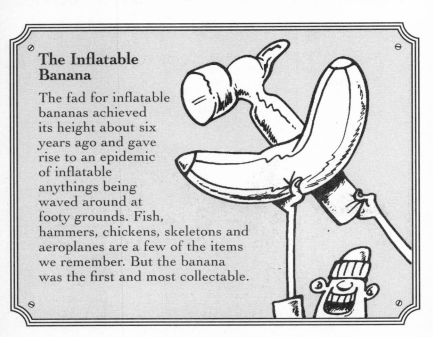

The **football rattle**, in days gone by, was an absolute must for every football fan in the land before its mysterious disappearance (see: *The Nutty Footy Book*, page 35).

Today, those rattles fetch serious dosh at auction, as frantic collectors outbid each other. We've had a quick think about what objects, seen frequently on the terraces, might become collectors' items in the future. So if you want to make a few bob, check out the Nutty Footy guide to future footy memorabilia!

The Inflatable Banana

The fad for inflatable bananas achieved its height about six years ago and gave rise to an epidemic of inflatable anythings being waved around at footy grounds. Fish, hammers, chickens, skeletons and aeroplanes are a few of the items we remember. But the banana was the first and most collectable.

The Big Sponge Finger

'nuff said!

Scouser Bubble Perm Wig and Moustache

After starting out as a comic sketch on *The Harry Enfield Show*, the 'calm down' scouser disguise kits began to be seen at football matches. Visiting fans wore them to Liverpool and Everton matches to rib-tickling effect.

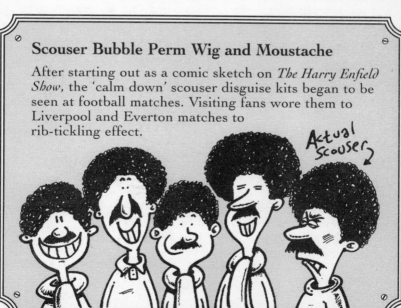

Actual Scouser

The European Air Horn

This item used to be heard only during European games. It has crept into the British scene over the past few years and remains a firm favourite. It should not be confused with other European items like The False Ref's Whistle, or The Full Salsa Band.

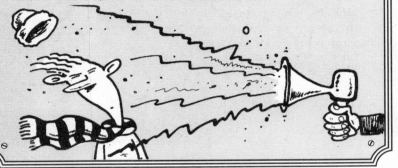

The Giant Banner

British banners used to be pathetic scraps of old tablecloth with 'Terry Yorath Is God' scrawled across them in biro. Not any more! Recently we have been seeing the magnificent Euro-style banners rippling across British footy fans' heads. The big clubs are the more common items. More collectable in future will be those banners seen at, say, Hartlepool or Torquay.

False Bellies

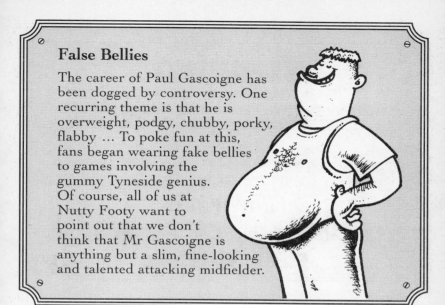

The career of Paul Gascoigne has been dogged by controversy. One recurring theme is that he is overweight, podgy, chubby, porky, flabby ... To poke fun at this, fans began wearing fake bellies to games involving the gummy Tyneside genius. Of course, all of us at Nutty Footy want to point out that we don't think that Mr Gascoigne is anything but a slim, fine-looking and talented attacking midfielder.

Recent picture from a poorly attended Torquay game demonstrates the problem of Giant Banners.

Olde Worlde Footie!

There are plenty of teams around (Hi, Newcastle!) who haven't won a carrot since before Jimmy Hill was a baby.

I know that's hard to imagine, so here's an artist's impression of what that may have looked like.

If you support one of those teams and yearn for the days when your side was slaughtering any side that crossed its path, now is your chance.

The brainy boffins in our Nutty labs have come up with the 'Nutty Footy Golden Age of Football Time Tunnel' (see advertising feature). But if you can't afford this top-notch bit of kit, don't despair! Try our *cut-price solution*. With the help of only a few household items (see pic.), a bit of hard work and a lot of imagination, you could be stepping out in some almost authentic 1930s' footy togs…

To recreate that authentic 'hairy shirt' feel, line a rough sack with a mixture of loft insulation and broken crisps…

… you can paint the 'shirt' in authentic team colours. (Remember, only use black and white paint; colour telly hadn't been invented then.)

Slap some marge on the bonce to get that shiny centre part just right!

Shorts were HUGE in the olden days, so simply take a pair of Granny's old bloomers and take the elastic out of the legs!

A couple of bricks tied to the toes feels just like those heavy iron-toecapped boots!

DIDN'T HE USED

We're all used to seeing footballers popping up on the telly as experts, or commenting on big games. But they can't <u>all</u> become the next Gary Lineker or Alan Hansen. We've delved into the Nutty Archives to find out some of the nuttier facts about the kind of things that footballers get up to after their final whistle has gone.

John Aston

who played for Manchester United from 1964 to 1981, now runs a pet shop!

THE UTTERLY NUTTY HISTORY OF FOOTY

Albert Bennet

formerly of Newcastle and Norwich, once sold whoopee cushions and stink bombs from a Lowestoft joke shop!

THE UTTERLY NUTTY HISTORY OF FOOTY

Gary Birtles

the million pound Forest and Man United player, left the game to flog fish!

THE UTTERLY NUTTY HISTORY OF FOOTY

Mike Channon

Southampton and England striker, is now a racehorse trainer!

THE UTTERLY NUTTY HISTORY OF FOOTY

John Chiedozie

used to play for Derby and Spurs. Now he supplies bouncy castles!

THE UTTERLY NUTTY HISTORY OF FOOTY

Bobby Sibbald

played for York, Leeds and Southport before moving to America, where he won the lottery!

THE UTTERLY NUTTY 🄽 HISTORY

Jim Fryatt

of Blackburn, Oldham and Charlton amongst others, once worked as a Las Vegas croupier!

Albert Gudmundsson

after playing for Arsenal amongst a number of clubs, became Iceland's Finance Minister!

THE UTTERLY NUTTY 🄽 HISTORY OF FOOTY

David Icke

the former Hereford and Coventry goalie, became a snooker commentator after retiring from football – before giving it all up for religion!

THE UTTERLY NUTTY 🄽 HISTORY OF

Mike Summerbee

former Man City winger, is now a shirt maker supplying Sly Stallone and David Bowie!

THE UTTERLY NUTTY 🄽 HISTORY OF FO

Ricky Villa

famously played for Spurs in the 1980s. He's now a cowboy in Argentina! (Actually, he owns a ranch...)

THE UTTERLY NUTTY 🄽 HISTORY OF FOOTY

Bobby Fisher

formerly of Orient, Cambridge United and Brentford, became a space alien! (Well – he appeared in the TV series Space Precinct after becoming an actor.)

THE UTTERLY NUTTY 🄽 HISTORY OF FOOTY

 FUTURE

Here we are on page 92 in the final moments of the book. The editor's checking his watch, Simon Bailey's checking his calculator, it looks as though he'll blow at any minute. There's just time to forget about history and take a peek into the distant future…

It's the year 7575. Human beings have continued to evolve. The brain has increased in size and power. Now players only have to **think** about playing, using alpha-thought-waves to control the ball. There is no need for players to develop muscles (except, obviously, Wimbledon players).

Crowds, of course, no longer need to attend games; they simply think about them. The Premiership has expanded to include not just teams from around the globe, but from around the universe.

FOOTY

Pictured below is a top-of-the-table clash between Athletico Macclesfield, the mega-succesful Champions of the Solar System, and Inter–HkjhYg//hgjjh&*56&yJYuty%$5432!@Eyt^%6uGhJjG-ghbgJJ FC, a team from the Western Universe Division. The beings on that planet have evolved along different lines from us. They resemble cheese and pickle sandwiches.

There is no need for a pitch, although some traditions are retained: the halftime pie, the halftime cup of tea, Alex Ferguson still moaning about something. Jimmy Hill is still on *Match of the Day* and Alan Hansen's great grandson is telling the viewers he's appalled at the defending.

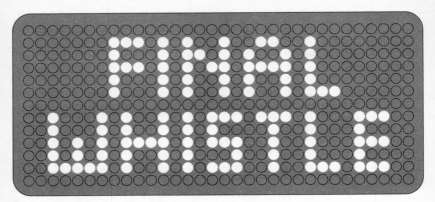

OK. That's it. The final whistle has blown. We are all Nuttied out. We have no more Nuttiness left. The Nuttiness is no more. All that is left to do is to swap shirts, go on a lap of honour and get interviewed in the tunnel by Gary Newbon.